THE BOOK OF
THUNKS®

Is not going fishing a hobby and other possibly impossible questions to stretch your brain and annoy your friends

Ian Gilbert

Foreword and Illustrations by Dr Andrew Curran

Crown House Publishing Limited
www.crownhouse.co.uk
www.crownhousepublishing.com

First published by

Crown House Publishing Ltd
Crown Buildings, Bancyfelin, Carmarthen, Wales, SA33 5ND, UK
www.crownhouse.co.uk

and

Crown House Publishing Company LLC
PO Box 2223, Williston, VT 05495 , USA
www.crownhousepublishing.com

First published 2008. Reprinted 2011, 2013, 2017.

British Library Cataloguing-in-Publication Data
A catalogue entry for this book is available
from the British Library.

Print ISBN 978-184590092-2
Mobi ISBN 978-184590233-9
ePub ISBN 978-184590313-8

LCCN 2008933131

Printed and bound in the UK by
Gomer Press, Llandysul, Ceredigion

To Phoebe

Whose engine is bigger than she is

Contents

Thunks and the Brain

Neurobiological science has identified that we carry all our thoughts, our feelings, even the core features of our personalities as hard-wired patterns of nerve cells called templates. These templates are stored in our brains, accessible by triggering the correct neurochemicals and delivering these to exactly the right nerve cells at exactly the right time. To change a template requires emotional commitment because the emotional part of our brains, the limbic system, controls not only learning but also attention. This is all achieved through the auspices of a neurochemical called dopamine, the main template-creating neurochemical in the brain.

Why is this relevant to this book of Thunks? Well, it is the templates that you have stored in your brain that this book is messing with. We all sit comfortably in our comfort zones, happy to feel and think and be the way we have always been. It's called complacency. It's probably the quickest way to get coronary artery disease, dissatisfied, and just plain bored than any other way I know. We sit there comfortably, *complacently* dying a little more each day because our templates are nicely formed by the interaction of our genetic potentials with our environment, and they say to us: It's fine. Just be as you are. Don't think differently. In fact, why bother thinking at all? Just accept you the way you are with all your misconceptions hard-wired into your brain. But experts in Alzheimer's Disease and other degenerative brain conditions are now saying that workouts that involve a mental challenge might be better for the brain than those that are routine.

This book will shake up your templates. It will rattle your thought routines. It will force you to think about things differently. It will, if used correctly, make you feel uncomfortable. And you never know, it might stave off that sense of complacency and that might keep your brain working longer and better.

Dr Andrew Curran
Consultant Neurologist
Alder Hey Children's Hospital

Instructions

1. Find a friend or family member

2. Ask a Thunk

3. Disagree with their answer*

4. Stand well back

5. Repeat

---

* For example if they say 'Of course there is such thing as "The French"' reply, 'So, who are they then?' They may respond that it is everyone living in France to which you reply 'What about in a hundred years when they are all dead? Will it still be "The French" then or will it be a new "The French"?' You get the idea...

HERE'S TO THUNKS!

THE
THUNKS

*Philosophy is the thinking science
hasn't got to yet...*

1. *Is there such a thing as 'The French'?*

2. If feeding a terrorist makes you a terrorist, does making them a cup of tea have the same effect?

3. IS NOT GOING FISHING A HOBBY?

4. If 0 degrees is a temperature, is 0 centimetres a height?

5. Can you love someone too much?

6. DOES A CLOUD DISPLACE SKY?

7. Can you turn a sound upside down?

8. If the cure for cancer meant constructing a huge factory in Antarctica, should we do it anyway?

9. IF YOU BELIEVE YOUR OWN LIES, ARE THEY LIES?

HE OPENED HIS WINDOW

10. Does opening a window change the size of a room?

11.   Is a broken-down car parked?

12.   IF YOU WERE BORN ON AN AEROPLANE IN GERMAN AIRSPACE ARE YOU GERMAN?

13.   Are you more of a success if you have had five top 40 hit records but no number ones compared to a one-hit wonder with one number one?

14. Is a cuckoo evil?

15. *Is there such a word as 'cope'?*

16. When you stand on a bridge are you standing on the ground?

17. IS A HORSE A VEHICLE?

18. Would it be OK to blast our rubbish into space?

19. *Would a baby born on a deserted island ever laugh?*

20. IS THE AIR IN YOUR LUNGS YOURS TO DO WITH WHAT YOU LIKE?

21. If I borrow a million pounds am I millionaire?

22. *Is a cloud in the sky (and not above, under, part of, or anything else)?*

23. If you found a contraceptive in your teenage daughter's room, should you be pleased?

24. COULD A FISH EXPRESS A PREFERENCE?

25. Can you say how many deaths it takes for them to become a statistic and not a tragedy?

26. IF A ROBOT WAITER BRINGS YOU A DRINK SHOULD YOU SAY THANK YOU?

27. Is a frozen pizza food?

28. *Can being in love be boring?*

29. When the roof is on the Millennium Stadium in Cardiff is it a room?

30. Would you rather live under democracy or under a dictatorship led by Father Christmas?

31.   Can you point to where the sky starts?

32. DO BOGEYS DISAPPEAR WHEN YOU FLICK THEM?

33. *Is there less 'outdoors' in the world every time someone builds a new conservatory?*

34. Does the depletion of fish stocks mitigate against the rise in sea levels?

35. SHOULD MPS BE MADE TO TRAVEL FIRST CLASS?

36. Will the planet weigh less when all the oil is used up?

37. DO YOU USE YOUR IMAGINATION WHEN YOU DREAM?

38. Can you get lost if you don't know where you're going?

39. *When you switch a light off does the part of the room nearest the bulb go dark first?*

40. Does the wind have a size?

41. IF YOU DO SOMETHING WRONG WHEN YOU ARE DRUNK SHOULD YOU FEEL LESS GUILTY THAN IF YOU HAD DONE IT STONE COLD SOBER?

42. *Is vandalising a speed camera the same as vandalising a lifebuoy by a river?*

IN THAT OUT-OF-THE-WAY PLACE,
THERE WAS NOWHERE ELSE TO GO.

43. Is it the same road in both directions?

44. IS TAPPING YOUR FINGERS TO
    MUSIC A FORM OF DANCE?

45. *If you have one chipped wine glass
    in the set should you use that one
    more than the others so that you
    don't chip them as well?*

46. Does giving to the poor
    encourage them to stay poor?

47. If some of your cells were in the body of
Vlad the Impaler, is part of you evil?

48. IS THE GAP BETWEEN THE NOTES MUSIC?

49. Can your mind hurt?

50. Would it be right for an African country to send money to the West to fund arts programmes?

51. *Should a terrorist just be called a murderer?*

52. DOES THE HORIZON BECOME HIGHER WHEN THE TIDE GOES OUT?

53. IS BLACK A COLOUR?

54. Can you think of two things at the same time?

55. WOULD YOU ACCEPT A HEART TRANSPLANT FROM A RAPIST?

56. Do bird nests have a design?

57. IF I DON'T NOTICE THE COW WHEN I DRIVE PAST IT, IS IT INVISIBLE?

58. *Could you ever 'not be happier'?*

59. Is the £10 yours before you take it out of the cash point?

60. Is it better to have loved and lost than never to have loved at all?

61. SHOULD WE BE ALLOWED TO HARPOON THE PETS OF JAPANESE PEOPLE FOR RESEARCH PURPOSES?

62. *Would you prefer a mobile phone that has amazing functionality but looks crap over one that looks stunning but just makes phone calls?*

63.   Can you bend air?

64. Would it be OK to stop the sea levels rising by dismantling Iceland?

65. IF YOU DON'T KNOW HOW CLEVER YOU ARE, ARE YOU STUPID?

66. Are the phrases 'cul8r' and 'see you later' the same thing?

67. COULD YOU KILL YOURSELF AS AN EXPERIMENT?

68. If a deciduous tree weighs more when it is in leaf does the UK weigh more in the summer?

69. *Is atheism a gift from God?*

70. IS IT WRONG IF
SOMEONE SWEARS AT
YOU IN A LANGUAGE
YOU DON'T
UNDERSTAND?

71. Is your diary of future plans more
important than your diary of things
you've done?

72. *If someone changed your life for
the better by lying to you, would
it be a good act?*

73. Is the journey from A to B the same journey in the dark?

74. Should the long-term unemployed be made to pick up the litter in the hedgerows?

75. IS NOT VOTING MORE A STATEMENT THAN A SIGN OF APATHY?

76. *If you were researching left-wing politics would you trust Wikipedia more than the Daily Mail?*

77. Can an animal be a murderer?

78. CAN YOU BE RACIST AGAINST YOUR OWN RACE?

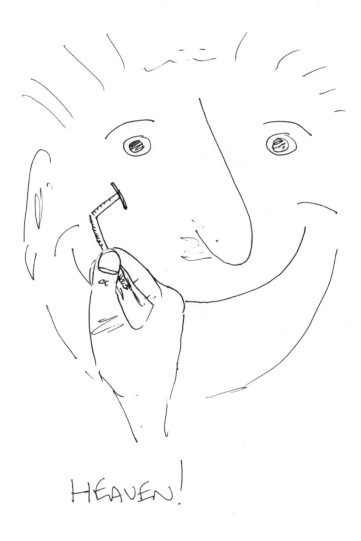

HEAVEN!

79. If you are easily pleased does that mean you will always get what you want?

80. Does an acorn contain more information than a computer?

81. COULD ONE WORD BE A BOOK?

82. If you paint a room does the room become smaller?

83. Does your soul get bigger as you grow?

84. IF YOU COULD SAVE THE PLANET BY WIPING OUT HALF THE POPULATION OF THE HUMAN RACE, SHOULD YOU?

85. Is there more future than past?

86. CAN A DUCK BE CONFUSED?

87. IS BEING MEDIOCRE
    A CHOICE?

88. *Should your estate own the e-mails in
    your inbox when you die?*

89. Do you have to have been
    unhappy to feel happy?

90. Is a ploughed field inside out?

91. *If you got to number one in the download chart by accident (say you called your band of lorry driver friends the Artic Monkeys) would you still be a success?*

92. If a doctor makes you wait half an hour have they given you 30 minutes (as opposed to taken 30 minutes)?

BILLY'S MUM SO WANTED
HIM TO BE HAPPY ON
HIS BIRTHDAY!

93. If you're happy to have a cake but sad
     when it's all gone, does that mean the
     more you eat the sadder you get?

94. If I turn the other cheek is it so that you won't see my cowardice?

95. *If a bear is chasing you and your friend, should you just run faster than your friend?*

96. IF YOU'VE LEFT YOUR LIGHTS ON AND FLATTENED YOUR BATTERY, WAS YOUR CAR BROKEN DOWN BEFORE YOU TRIED TO START IT?

97. DO RICH PEOPLE HAVE
BETTER TASTE THAN POOR
PEOPLE?

98. Do you need a vicar to stop a
church being a church?

99. *Is it OK to bring the law from your
country into someone else's?*

100. Can you steal from yourself?

101. *Does completing a dot-to-dot puzzle make you an artist?*

102. SHOULD FOOD BE CHEAPER FOR POOR PEOPLE?

103. Does your house weigh more the dustier it gets?

104. Is it easier to make someone else think something than feel something?

105. Is it better to feel safe when you're at risk than to be safe but not feel it?

106. Does the farmer own the pollen coming from his crops?

107. IS IT BETTER TO SPEND MONEY ON SAVING A THREATENED ENVIRONMENT RATHER THAN ON SAVING THE ANIMALS IN IT?

108. *If a yacht is sailing at three knots into a tide travelling in the opposite direction at three knots, is the yacht moving?*

109.	IF IT'S OK TO HAVE FOOTWEAR THAT HELPS
	IMPROVE YOUR PERFORMANCE IN THE
	OLYMPICS, IS IT OK TO HAVE A PROSTHETIC
	LEG THAT HELPS YOU RUN FASTER?

110.	*Is a hovering bird flying?*

111.	Should you pronounce French words
	used in English with a French
	accent (especially when they are 'le
	mot just')?

112. If something makes you happy, will it happening twice make you twice as happy?

113. Does electricity weigh anything?

114. CAN YOU IMAGINE A SMELL?

115. Should we pay drug addicts to stay clean?

116. **SHOULD STUPID PEOPLE BE PREVENTED FROM VOTING?**

117. *If I paint over a window is it still a window?*

118. **Is a tree made of wood?**

119. Is buying brain-enhancing drugs or software for your children to help them do better in their exams a form of cheating?

120. IF YOU DON'T RUN OVER THAT RABBIT, HAVE YOU SAVED ITS LIFE?

121. Can you choose to feel excited?

122. *Does lined paper weigh more than blank paper?*

123. IF YOU HAD ONLY EVER LIVED IN A BOX COULD YOU IMAGINE ANYTHING OTHER THAN THE INSIDE OF A BOX?

124. Are problems inevitable?

125. *Does time exist?*

126. Does the flashing light from a lighthouse flash?

127. ARE 'FACTS' THAT TURN OUT TO BE WRONG STILL PART OF YOUR KNOWLEDGE?

128.   IF McDONALDS SPENT BILLIONS RESCUING
       THE TIGER FROM EXTINCTION SHOULD THEY
       THEN BE ALLOWED TO SELL McTIGER
       BURGERS?

129.   *Would you rather be a dead celebrity or a living criminal?*

130.   Is driving 10 mph over the speed
       limit ten times worse than driving
       one mile over the speed limit?

THE TURNER ART PRIZE

THEY ALL AGREED IT WAS BETTER THAN THAT BLOODY BED. OR THE BEAR COME TO THAT.

131. Are skid marks art?

132.   You're standing at the foot of Mont
       Blanc — is the top of the mountain
       further away than London?

133.   Is it best to have the best person
       for the job as opposed to the most
       local person for the job?

134.   ARE THERE MORE
       COLOURS THAN
       THINGS?

135. Can you make someone else feel
something?

136. TRIGGER'S BROOM HAD SEVENTEEN NEW HEADS AND FOURTEEN NEW HANDLES BUT WAS IT STILL THE SAME BROOM?

137. Would you give blood to save the life of a paedophile?

138. Are there different types of sadness?

139. *Could I publish a book of blank pages and copyright it?*

140.   Do you choose your personality?

141.   *Is whistling a form of singing?*

142.   WHEN YOU READ A BOOK, ARE
THE THOUGHTS GOING THROUGH
YOUR HEAD YOURS (AS OPPOSED
TO THE AUTHOR'S)?

143. If a urinal is a work of art, was it a
work of art before the artist first
laid eyes on it?

144. Is everyone capable of evil
acts?

145. DOES A MIGRATING BUTTERFLY
KNOW ITS WAY?

146. *Do you own your own poo?*

BOB THOUGHT HE MIGHT SELL THE ~~IDEA~~ TO IKEA.

147. If you keep flowers in a skip, is the skip a vase?

148. *Swans mate for life so could you say they are in love?*

149. COULD ONE ARMY OF ROBOTS FIGHTING ANOTHER ARMY OF ROBOTS EVER DECIDE A WAR?

150. If you give me 50p by throwing it at me but I don't catch it and it goes down the drain, who has lost 50p?

151. Do you love each child as much whether you have one, three or eight?

152. COULD A COMPUTER WRITE A POEM?

153. Can I say I've been to Amsterdam if I drove through it asleep in a bus?

154. *Is space something?*

155. Does your dog think about you when you're at work?

156. IF YOU DECIDE TO ONLY EVER CHOOSE THE EASY OPTION, ARE YOU MAKING LIFE HARD FOR YOURSELF?

157. *Can air get wet?*

158. CAN A FACT BE RIGHT AND WRONG AT THE SAME TIME?

159. *Is it more of a failure to fail to get to the top of the mountain and come home safely than to reach the summit but die on the way back down?*

160. Can you guarantee for sure that a flashing light is working?

161. *If you'd have spent more time learning to play the piano at school than you did learning algebra, would you be spending more time playing the piano now than you do using algebra?*

162. # ARE WE MORE ALIVE THAN A TREE?

163. Do people with good memories have the best imaginations?

HE HAD TO STOP THINKING OF ELEPHANTS.

164. Are thoughts things?

165. *Could someone steal your rubbish from you?*

166. **COULD YOU GIVE UP RELIGION FOR LENT?**

167. Is an official executioner a murderer?

168. WOULD YOU RATHER A FAMILY MEMBER MARRIED A TRAFFIC WARDEN THAN A MILLIONAIRE CON ARTIST?

ANOTHER FAMILY TORN APART

BY THE FLAT-PACK BLUES

169. If you fail to put up an Ikea wardrobe despite trying to follow the instructions, is it their fault or yours?

170. *Is a tunnel through a mountain below ground?*

171. Could Take That do a Take That tribute band?

172. ARE THERE ANY SOUNDS NOT YET HEARD?

173. IS NOT LIKING HAIRY
ARMPITS ON A WOMAN AS
NATURAL AS HAIRY ARMPITS
ON A WOMAN?

174. Can you stand on the
same beach twice?

175. *Should we spend billions to protect ourselves
from the possibility of an asteroid impact
whilst there are people dying from infected
drinking water?*

176. *Should you be polite to criminals?*

177. Is the future closer than it was this time last year?

178. DOES A GEOSTATIONARY SATELLITE HOVER?

THE SHADOW BULLIES
WERE BACK!

179. Are shadows things?

180.   IF A HEALTHY PERSON, WHO
       COULD SAVE FIVE PEOPLE BY
       DONATING ALL THEIR ORGANS,
       WALKED INTO A HOSPITAL ASKING
       FOR DIRECTIONS, SHOULD THE
       DOCTOR KILL THEM?

181.   When the automatic hand
       drier fails to work, does it
       fail to work automatically?

182.   *Do you own the space in your pockets?*

183. When you eat an egg are you eating a bird?

184. If a Rolls Royce were dangling above a canyon by a thread, would the thread be more valuable than the Rolls Royce?

185. DO YOU LOVE A FAMILY MEMBER LESS AFTER THEY HAVE DIED?

186. *Would a Martian know a beautiful woman if it saw one?*

187. Is there anything that isn't science?

188. DOES THE WORLD WEIGH MORE WHEN IT'S RAINING?

189. IF YOU WERE ARRESTED
FOR BEING HAPPY WOULD
THERE BE ENOUGH
EVIDENCE TO CONVICT
YOU?

190. Is it better to do your best and lose
than it is to perform below par and
win?

191. *Is computer hacking a form
of terrorism?*

192. ARE YOU JUST AS ALIVE
WHEN YOU'RE ASLEEP AS YOU
ARE WHEN YOU'RE AWAKE?

193. Can you touch the wind?

194. *Is guilt an act as opposed to an emotion?*

GEORGE SWAM INTO
A PUDDLE OF AIR

195. Can you have a puddle of air?

196. Can science tell you whether something is beautiful?

197. IF RELIGION WERE BANNED WOULD THERE BE MORE GOOD IN THE WORLD?

198. *Do you know what the worst thing that can happen is?*

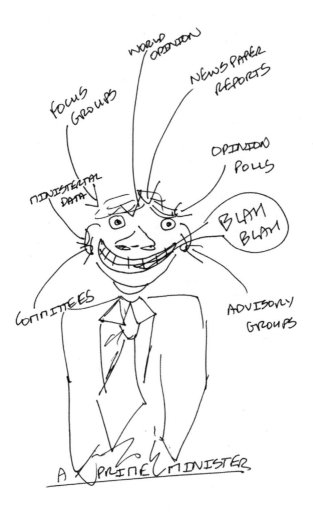

199.   Can you have no imagination?

200. ## WILL IT EVER BE OK TO HAVE SEX WITH A ROBOT (IF IT ISN'T ALREADY)?

201. Do we have our parents to thank for who we are?

202. If a waiter leaves an item off the bill and you say nothing, is that stealing?

203. *Can we ever really know if we are more intelligent than a dolphin?*

204. Does a unicorn have more horns than a pixie?

205. DO BOGEYS SMELL?

206. IS BEING A FOOTBALLER'S WIFE A CAREER?

207. Does the new leaf come from inside the tree?

208. CAN YOU DESIGN SOMETHING WITH TWO WHEELS, PEDALS AND A SEAT THAT ISN'T A BICYCLE?

IT WAS A SURPRISINGLY QUILK READ.

209. If you typed the word 'run' a thousand times would that be a short story?

210.   Can you identify the point where your lap starts?

211.   CAN YOU SAY FOR SURE THAT THERE WILL BE A SCRUM IN THE RUGBY MATCH THAT'S JUST STARTED?

212.   *Is a bat more of a bird than a penguin is?*

213.   CAN A SQUIRREL EVER TRULY
       BE HAPPY?

214.   If you employ someone, do you own
       them (or a part of them)?

215.   Is a valley more of a space
       than a thing?

216. RATHER THAN APOLOGISING FOR SOMETHING WE DIDN'T PERSONALLY DO HUNDREDS OF YEARS BEFORE WE WERE BORN, SHOULD WE JUST GIVE LIVERPOOL TO AFRICA AND CALL IT QUITS?

217. *Are you sure your pets don't talk about you when you leave the house?*

218. IS MISERY INFECTIOUS?

219.   Do crows know they all look the same?

220.   # ARE YOU A DIFFERENT PERSON BY THE END OF EACH DAY?

221.   Could you ever learn too much?

222. WOULD YOU BE
HAPPY IF YOU HAD
ALL YOU WANTED?

223. Is it easier to remember something
wonderful than to forget something
horrible?

224. Is toast made of bread?

225. Is a static caravan a caravan?

226. If you only ever made love to one person all your life, would you know if you had missed out?

227. CAN YOU HATE HAVING FUN?

228. Is any belief a form of madness?

PEPE, THE MEXICAN JUMPING
BEAN, LOVED TO LIVE TO
THE MAXxx.

229. If you find a foreign body in your mouth
when eating, is it better that you do know
what it is (as opposed to not knowing its
identity)?

230. *If I laugh at a joke but you don't, was the joke funny?*

231. CAN YOU TOUCH A REFLECTION?

232. IS IT A ROMANTIC GESTURE TO BUY SOMEONE FLOWERS ON VALENTINE'S DAY?

233. Can water get wet?

234. *Could anything with a brain have a headache?*

235. IS A TRANSLATION OF A BOOK AN IMITATION?

236.   If you gave a fish a million pounds would it be rich?

237.   *If your name is part of who you are, would someone with the same name as you have a similar identity?*

238.   DOES A SKYLARK EVER GET OUT OF BREATH WHEN IT FLIES AND SINGS AT THE SAME TIME?

239. MUST YOU HAVE KNOWN DEFEAT TO BE ABLE TO REALLY SUCCEED?

240. Should walking across hot coals be part of the school curriculum?

241. Is it worse to slap a child or to torture a cat?

242. If cows evolved to be cleverer should we stop eating them?

243. *Is it wrong to think about having sex with the vicar?*

244. CAN YOU BE AFRAID OF FAIRIES?

BILL'S NEW MARKETING
PLOY LEFT EVERYTHING TO
THE IMAGINATION.

245. Can a white square on a white background
be a logo?

246. *Is illegible handwriting with good spelling better than neat handwriting with poor spelling?*

247. WOULD THE MODERN WORLD COME TO A HALT IF MESSRS GATES, BRANSON, MURDOCH, BUFFET, DYSON, PAGE AND BRYN WENT ON STRIKE?

248. CAN YOU BE MADE TO BELIEVE IN GOD?

249. If I read a magazine in a shop without paying for it, is that stealing?

250. *Is darts more of a sport than ice dancing?*

251. *Does a sphere start and end in exactly the same place?*

252. If it was proven that God exists, would you still be able to believe in Him (or Her)?

253. IF PEOPLE DISPLACE AIR, WHERE HAS ALL THE DISPLACED AIR GONE NOW THAT THERE ARE MORE PEOPLE ON EARTH THAN AT ANY OTHER TIME?

THE TURNER PRIZE

THE EYES FOLLOWED
THEM EVEN IF
THEY MOVED.

254. If you draw a random squiggle that
happens to look like a face, have you
drawn a face?

255. Would a baby born on a deserted island know right from wrong?

256. CAN YOU KNOW SOMETHING WITHOUT KNOWING THAT YOU KNOW IT?

257. Is it better to seek forgiveness than ask permission?

258. SHOULD ENTREPRENEURS BE ALLOWED TO PAY LESS TAX THAN INVESTMENT BANKERS BECAUSE OF ALL THE JOBS AND OPPORTUNITIES THEY HAVE CREATED OUT OF NOTHING?

259. *Could you get some sky into your pocket?*

260. Does your desk say more about you than your car?

261. *Is photocopying art?*

262. Would it be suicide if I chose not to get out of the way of a runaway bus?

263. CAN YOU TASTE YOUR OWN TASTE BUDS?

264. DOES READING THE DAILY PAPER MEAN YOU DON'T HAVE TO THINK FOR YOURSELF?

265. *Would it be wrong to have sex with a dog in an online virtual world?*

266. Can a colour make you sad?

267. **IF YOU HAVE A PSYCHIATRIC CONDITION THAT MAKES YOU DO BAD THINGS, ARE YOU A BAD PERSON?**

268. *Can you spot the moment that a clap becomes a round of applause?*

269. Do you need to be an artist to turn a pile of bricks into a work of art (or can anyone do it)?

270.   If you swallow an oyster can you say it has been eaten if it is still alive?

271. Would you be a different
person if you'd chosen a
different career?

272. Is a fable truer than a newspaper?

273. WOULD YOU GIVE MONEY TO A
BUSKER PLAYING THE
TRIANGLE PART FROM YOUR
FAVOURITE MOZART PIECE?

274. *Is racism natural?*

275.   *If you watch a play where the second half is the same as the first half, have you seen one play or two?*

276.   IF GENETIC RESEARCH IDENTIFIES THAT YOU HAVE A CONDITION THAT MEANS YOU WILL DIE IN TEN YEARS, SHOULD YOU BE TOLD, WHETHER YOU WANT TO KNOW OR NOT?

277.   **IS BEER POROUS?**

278.   Is a scientist with a physics degree cleverer than the bloke who fixes your car?

279. *Is it OK for your job to be really boring if it pays well?*

280. IF I HOLD MY MOBILE PHONE VIDEO SCREEN CLOSE TO MY FACE WILL IT BE THE SAME SIZE AS A WIDESCREEN TV ON THE OTHER SIDE OF THE ROOM?

281. Is a football hooligan a type of warrior?

282.   Can an ant see a mountain?

283.   CAN YOU INSULT SOMEONE
       POLITELY?

284.   Does the front of a
       firework look the same as
       the back?

285.   *Is a circus without animals a circus (as
       opposed to just a show)?*

NOOOO!

HECTOR HAD HAD ENOUGH!

286. Could you make a duck sad?

287. Assuming you wouldn't be allowed to stand in a pub and smoke with your head out of the window, would it be OK to stand outside a pub and smoke with your head inside the window?

288. IF SOMEONE ASKS YOU A QUESTION, IS GIVING A FACT AS THE ANSWER BETTER THAN GIVING AN OPINION, WHICH IS BETTER THAN SAYING YOU DON'T KNOW?

289. *Is it OK to be for abortion but against the death penalty?*

290.   *Does Homer Simpson exist?*

291.   If scientists can create
       living things that are part
       animal, part human, is
       such a thing more human
       than a 'baby' in the womb
       that is just two cells big?

292.   COULD YOU EVER GET A MIRROR NOT
       TO WORK (WITHOUT BREAKING IT)?

293.   If I met you a year ago on the third floor of a building that has now been knocked down, where is the spot where I met you now?

294.   IF BOTH HANDS FALL OFF YOUR FAVOURITE CLOCK, IS IT STILL A CLOCK?

295.   *Does a cup of tea weigh more when you add a spoonful of sugar?*

296.   Can you ever really live up to your full potential?

HERMAN AND GRUBBENFUELER
LIKED THEIR JOB OF LOOKING
AFTER LOST STONES.

297. If you lose a stone on a diet could you say
where the stone has gone?

298. COULD ANYONE PROVE YOU WRONG IF YOU CLAIM THAT YOU CAN MAKE TRAFFIC LIGHTS CHANGE FROM RED TO GREEN JUST BY STARING AT THEM?

299. Is it ever possible to learn nothing?

300. *If your partner points out a parking space in a crowded car park but when you get there there's one of those annoying little cars in it, but next to it there is a space neither of you had seen, were they right or wrong in saying there was a space there?*

Enjoyed playing around with
the *Thunks* in this book?

Feel free to share some of your own.

www.thunks.co.uk

The Compleat Thunks® Book

Ian Gilbert

ISBN 978-178135272-4

A brain workout book for uncertain times.

We are living in a world where facts don't count, certainty no longer exists and complexity means we never quite know what will happen next. To prepare ourselves better for such a world, we need a brain workout that isn't so much about finding answers as getting our heads around questions.

We need *The Compleat Thunks® Book*.

In *The Compleat Thunks® Book*, Thunks® creator Ian Gilbert brings together Thunks® from a number of his books as well as over 100 new ones, all designed to get you thinking, questioning, debating and arguing your way to a better understanding of how to survive in a world gone dangerously bonkers.

Some of these Thunks® appear in *The Book of Thunks®*, ISBN 978-184590092-2 and *The Little Book of Thunks®*, ISBN 978-184590062-5.